301 Brilliant Facts: Space and Aliens Edition

M.K. Publishing House

Copyright © [2024] by [M.K. Publishing House]

All rights reserved.

No portion of this book may be reproduced in any form without written permission from the publisher or author, except as permitted by U.S. copyright law.

Contents

1. The Big Bang and the Birth of the Universe — 1
2. The Sun: Our Cosmic Super Star — 12
3. Planets: The Wild and Wonderful Worlds in Our Solar System — 22
4. Moons: More Than Earth's Night Light — 32
5. Asteroids, Comets, and Meteors: Space Rocks on the Move! — 42
6. Aliens: Are We Alone in the Universe? — 52
7. Black Holes: The Universe's Most Mysterious Monsters — 62
8. Galaxies: Giant Star Cities Across the Universe — 72

9. Spaceships and Rovers: Exploring the Final Frontier   82

10. Becoming a Space Explorer: Your Future in the Stars   92

Chapter One

The Big Bang and the Birth of the Universe

1. Imagine the whole universe starting as a tiny, super-hot dot smaller than the period at the end of this sentence! That's how scientists think everything began about 13.8 billion years ago. This tiny dot suddenly grew super fast, like blowing up a balloon, and that's what we call the Big Bang!

2. Before the Big Bang, there was nothing - no stars, no planets, not even space or time! It's hard to imagine, right? It's like trying to think about what's outside the universe. Our brains get all mixed up because we're used to thinking about things inside the universe, not before it existed!

3. The Big Bang wasn't actually a "bang" like an explosion. It was more like everything suddenly stretching out super fast, kind of like when you pull a stretched-out slinky toy really quickly. Scientists call this quick stretching "inflation," and it happened faster than you can blink your eyes!

4. Right after the Big Bang, the universe was so hot that not even atoms could form. It was like a super-hot soup of tiny particles zooming around really fast. If you could touch it (which you couldn't!), it would be way hotter than the hottest oven you can imagine.

5. As the universe grew bigger, it started to cool down. After about 380,000 years (which is a long time for us but short for the universe), it was cool enough for the first atoms to form. These were mostly hydrogen atoms, the simplest kind of atom there is.

6. The first light in the universe appeared about 380,000 years after the Big Bang. Scientists call this the "cosmic microwave background radiation." It's like an echo of the Big Bang that we can still see today with special telescopes. It's the oldest light in the universe!

7. For millions of years after the Big Bang, the universe was dark. There were no stars or galaxies yet, just clouds of gas floating in space. Scientists call this time the "cosmic dark ages." It's like the universe was waiting for something exciting to happen!

8. About 100 million years after the Big Bang, the first stars started to form. These stars were huge, much bigger than our Sun, and they lit up the dark universe for the first time. It must have been an amazing light show!

9. The first stars were made mostly of hydrogen and helium, the simplest elements. But inside these stars, other elements like carbon, oxygen, and iron were created. When the stars exploded, they spread these new elements into space. That's where all the stuff that makes up Earth came from!

10. Galaxies started forming about 400 million years after the Big Bang. They looked different from galaxies today - they were smaller and more irregular. Over time, galaxies grew by crashing into each other and joining together, like cosmic bumper cars!

11. Our own galaxy, the Milky Way, formed about 13.6 billion years ago, not too long after the Big Bang. It's been growing and changing ever since. When you look at the stars at night, you're seeing part of our huge galaxy!

12. The Sun and Earth didn't form until about 9 billion years after the Big Bang. That means the universe was already really old when our solar system was born. It's like we're the new kids on the cosmic block!

13. Scientists figured out the universe is expanding by looking at faraway galaxies. They saw that almost all galaxies are moving away from us, like raisins in a rising loaf of bread. This was a big clue that helped them discover the Big Bang!

14. The stuff we see - stars, planets, and galaxies - is only a tiny part of what's in the universe. Most of

the universe is made of mysterious things called dark matter and dark energy. Scientists are still trying to figure out what these are!

15. If you could travel back in time to see the Big Bang, you'd need a really fast time machine! You'd have to go back about 13.8 billion years. That's so long ago that if each year was just one second, you'd be traveling for over 400 years!

16. Right after the Big Bang, the universe was expanding faster than the speed of light! But don't worry, this doesn't break any rules. It was space itself that was stretching, not things moving through space. It's like drawing dots on a balloon and blowing it up - the dots move apart!

17. The early universe was so hot that the tiniest particles, called quarks, couldn't even stick together

to form bigger particles. It was like trying to build a sandcastle when the sand is too hot to touch!

18. About one second after the Big Bang, the universe cooled enough for quarks to join together and form protons and neutrons. These are the building blocks of atoms. It's amazing to think that all the atoms in your body were born just one second after the universe began!

19. For the first 380,000 years, the universe was like a glowing fog. Light couldn't travel far without bumping into particles. When atoms finally formed, light could travel freely for the first time. It was like the universe suddenly became see-through!

20. The Big Bang theory was first proposed by a scientist named Georges Lemaître in the 1920s. He imagined the universe starting as a "cosmic egg" that

exploded. People thought it was a crazy idea at first, but later scientists found evidence that he was right!

21. One piece of evidence for the Big Bang is that we can see galaxies moving away from us in all directions. It's like we're in the middle of a giant cosmic firework that's still exploding, even after billions of years!

22. Another clue that supports the Big Bang theory is the amount of helium in the universe. Scientists can calculate how much helium should have been created in the Big Bang, and it matches what we see in space. It's like solving a giant cosmic puzzle!

23. The Big Bang created equal amounts of matter and antimatter. Antimatter is like matter's opposite twin - when they touch, they disappear in a flash of energy! Somehow, a tiny bit more matter survived, and that's what made everything we see today.

24. If you could watch the universe grow from the beginning until now, sped up so that each billion years took one second, the whole history of the universe would take less than 14 seconds! Our entire human history would happen in the last tiny fraction of a second.

25. The universe is still expanding today, and it's actually speeding up! Scientists don't know why, but they think it might be because of dark energy. It's like the universe is a balloon that's being blown up faster and faster.

26. In the very early universe, all four fundamental forces of nature (gravity, electromagnetism, strong nuclear force, and weak nuclear force) might have been one single force. As the universe cooled, they split apart, like friends going their separate ways.

27. The Big Bang didn't happen in one place in space - it happened everywhere at once! Every point in the universe was once squished together with every other point. It's hard to imagine, but that means the Big Bang happened right where you're sitting now!

28. Some scientists think our universe might be just one of many universes, like bubbles in a giant cosmic bubble bath. This idea is called the "multiverse." If it's true, the Big Bang might have been just one of many big bangs!

29. The early universe went through different stages, each with a funny name. There was the "quark epoch," the "hadron epoch," and even the "photon epoch." It's like the universe was growing up and going through different phases, just like we do!

30. Even though the Big Bang happened so long ago, scientists can still study it today. They use powerful

telescopes, super-fast computers, and even particle colliders that recreate conditions like the early universe. It's like being a detective solving the biggest mystery of all time!

Chapter Two

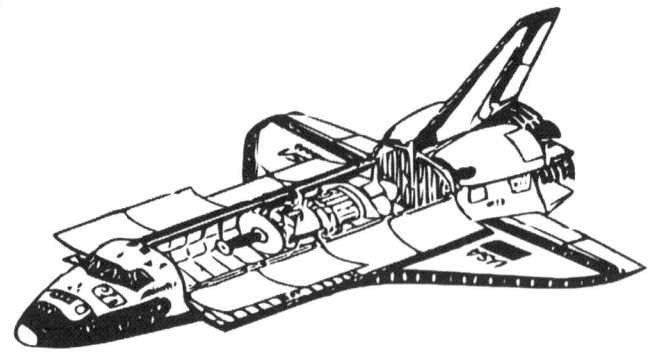

The Sun: Our Cosmic Super Star

1. The Sun is like a giant space light bulb that never turns off! It's so big that more than a million Earths could fit inside it. Imagine trying to play hide and seek in a ball that big! The Sun is so huge that it makes up 99.8% of everything in our solar system.

2. Our Sun is actually a star, just like the ones you see at night. But it looks bigger and brighter because

it's much closer to us than other stars. It's like having a firefly in your room versus seeing one far away in your backyard - the close one seems much brighter!

3. The Sun is super hot! The center is about 27 million degrees Fahrenheit. That's way hotter than your oven at home. If you could touch the Sun (which you can't!), it would be like touching a million hot stoves all at once. Ouch!

4. The Sun is so bright that it can hurt your eyes if you look at it directly. That's why we wear sunglasses outside. It's like the Sun is playing a game of "staring contest" with Earth, and the Sun always wins!

5. The Sun doesn't have a solid surface like Earth. It's made of hot gas all the way through. If you tried to stand on the Sun, you'd fall right through it! It's like trying to stand on a giant ball of really hot Jell-O in space.

6. The Sun is about 93 million miles away from Earth. That's so far that it would take you 177 years to get there in a car going 60 miles per hour. You'd need to pack a lot of snacks for that road trip!

7. Light from the Sun takes about 8 minutes to reach Earth. So when you see the Sun, you're actually seeing what it looked like 8 minutes ago! It's like watching a TV show with an 8-minute delay.

8. The Sun is about 4.6 billion years old. That's older than any dinosaur fossil! If the Sun's life was a day, Earth would only show up around 3 PM, and humans would appear in the last second before midnight. We're like the Sun's new baby!

9. The Sun will keep shining for about 5 billion more years. After that, it will turn into a big red ball called a red giant. Then it will shrink down to a tiny, dim

star called a white dwarf. It's like the Sun is going through its own life stages, just very slowly!

10. The Sun doesn't just give us light - it also gives us heat. Without the Sun, Earth would be a frozen ball of ice! The Sun is like a giant space heater keeping our planet cozy and warm.

11. The Sun spins around, just like Earth does! But because it's made of gas, different parts spin at different speeds. The middle spins faster than the top and bottom. It's like a weird merry-go-round where the horses in the middle go faster!

12. The Sun has dark spots on it called sunspots. These are cooler areas on the Sun's surface. Even though they look dark, they're still super bright - about as bright as the full moon! It's like the Sun has freckles that come and go.

13. The Sun shoots out huge bursts of energy called solar flares. These can cause pretty lights in the sky on Earth called auroras. It's like the Sun is putting on a colorful light show for us!

14. The Sun makes a humming sound, but we can't hear it on Earth. Scientists use special instruments to listen to it. If we could hear it, it would sound like a deep, low hum. It's like the Sun is singing a very low note all the time!

15. The Sun is mostly made of hydrogen and helium, the two lightest elements. But it also has tiny amounts of heavier stuff like gold and iron. It's like a giant cosmic soup with a sprinkle of valuable ingredients!

16. The Sun's gravity is what keeps Earth and all the other planets orbiting around it. Without the Sun,

the planets would just float away into space! It's like the Sun is the center of a giant space merry-go-round.

17. The Sun doesn't rise or set - that's just how it looks from Earth because our planet is spinning. If you could watch from space, you'd see that the Sun stays still while Earth turns. It's like we're on a giant carousel going around the Sun!

18. The energy from the Sun helps plants grow through a process called photosynthesis. Plants use sunlight to make their own food! It's like the Sun is a giant chef cooking meals for all the plants on Earth.

19. The Sun doesn't have rings like Saturn or moons like Jupiter. It's the only object in our solar system that makes its own light. All the other things we see in the sky are just reflecting the Sun's light, like mirrors in space!

20. The Sun is actually moving through space! Our whole solar system is traveling around the center of our galaxy, the Milky Way. We're moving at about 450,000 miles per hour! It's like we're on a super-fast cosmic train.

21. The Sun has different layers, just like an onion. The part we see is called the photosphere. Above that is the chromosphere, and the outer layer is called the corona. It's like the Sun is wearing a bunch of invisible coats!

22. Sometimes the Moon passes in front of the Sun, causing a solar eclipse. For a few minutes, day turns into night! It's like the Moon and Sun are playing a giant game of peek-a-boo in the sky.

23. The Sun is a yellow dwarf star, but it's not really yellow! From space, it looks white. It only appears yellow from Earth because of our atmosphere. It's

like Earth is wearing yellow sunglasses that change how we see the Sun!

24. The Sun is so powerful that in just one second, it produces enough energy to power the United States for 9 million years! That's more energy than all the power plants on Earth could make in a million years. Talk about a super-powered star!

25. The Sun's surface is always bubbling and boiling. Hot gas rises up, cools off, and sinks back down. It looks like a pot of soup boiling on the stove, but much, much bigger! These bubbles are called granules, and they're each about the size of Texas!

26. The Sun has a powerful magnetic field that flips every 11 years. When this happens, the Sun's north pole becomes its south pole, and vice versa. It's like the Sun is playing a cosmic game of flip-flop!

27. If you could cut the Sun in half (which you can't!), you'd see it has layers like an onion. The core is in the middle, then the radiative zone, then the convection zone, and finally the surface we see. It's like a giant space jawbreaker candy!

28. The Sun doesn't have a solid surface to walk on, but if it did, you'd weigh about 28 times more there than on Earth! A 50-pound kid would weigh 1,400 pounds on the Sun. That's heavier than a cow!

29. The Sun is actually a big nuclear reactor. It smashes tiny particles together to make energy. This is called nuclear fusion. It's like the Sun is playing a never-ending game of atomic bumper cars to make light and heat!

30. Ancient people used to think the Sun was a god because it was so powerful and important. They didn't know it was just a big ball of hot gas! Now we

know better, but the Sun is still super amazing and important for life on Earth.

Chapter Three

Planets: The Wild and Wonderful Worlds in Our Solar System

1. Our solar system is like a big family of planets, with the Sun as the parent. We have eight planets: Mer-

cury, Venus, Earth, Mars, Jupiter, Saturn, Uranus, and Neptune. Each planet is unique, with its own special features. It's like a cosmic playground where each planet has its own personality!

2. Mercury is the closest planet to the Sun. It's super hot during the day and freezing cold at night! The temperature can change by 1,100 degrees Fahrenheit in one day. That's like going from a really hot oven to a giant freezer in just a few hours!

3. Venus is called Earth's twin because it's about the same size as our planet. But it's not a friendly twin! Venus is super hot, with thick clouds made of acid. If you could stand on Venus, it would be like being in a really stinky oven!

4. Earth is the only planet we know that has life. It's just right - not too hot, not too cold. We have water,

air, and everything living things need. Earth is like the "Goldilocks" planet - it's just right for us!

5. Mars is called the Red Planet because it looks reddish-orange. It has the biggest volcano in the solar system, called Olympus Mons. This volcano is three times taller than Mount Everest! It's like a giant space mountain that would take forever to climb.

6. Jupiter is the biggest planet in our solar system. It's so big that more than 1,300 Earths could fit inside it! Jupiter also has a giant storm called the Great Red Spot. This storm is bigger than Earth and has been going on for hundreds of years!

7. Saturn is famous for its beautiful rings. These rings are made of millions of pieces of ice and rock, some as big as houses! If you could stand on Saturn, you'd feel very light because it's made mostly of gas.

It would be like bouncing on a giant space trampoline!

8. Uranus is tilted on its side, so its seasons are super weird. One pole faces the Sun for 42 years of summer, then the other pole gets 42 years of winter. Imagine having summer vacation for 42 years straight!

9. Neptune is the windiest planet in our solar system. Its winds can blow up to 1,200 miles per hour! That's five times faster than the strongest hurricane on Earth. If you were on Neptune, you'd be blown away like a feather in a super strong wind!

10. Pluto used to be called a planet, but now scientists call it a dwarf planet. It's smaller than our Moon! Pluto is so far away that the Sun looks like just a bright star from there. It's like the shy kid at the edge of the solar system playground.

11. Mercury spins really slowly. One day on Mercury lasts about 59 Earth days! But it zips around the Sun super fast. If you lived on Mercury, you'd only have about 88 Earth days in a year. That's like having your birthday party every three months!

12. Venus spins backwards compared to most other planets. On Venus, the Sun rises in the west and sets in the east. It's like the planet is doing a backwards somersault all the time! A day on Venus is longer than its year - how silly is that?

13. Earth is the only planet not named after a god or goddess. All the other planets have fancy names from Roman myths, but Earth just means "ground" in old English. It's like if you named your pet dog "Dog" while all your friends gave their pets fancy names!

14. Mars has two tiny moons named Phobos and Deimos. They're so small that they look like potatoes

floating in space! Phobos is slowly getting closer to Mars and might crash into it one day. It's like a game of cosmic catch that's lasting millions of years!

15. Jupiter has at least 79 moons! The four biggest ones are called the Galilean moons, named after the scientist who discovered them. One of these moons, Europa, might have an ocean under its icy surface. It's like Jupiter has its own mini solar system!

16. Saturn's rings are super thin. Even though they're wider than the distance between Earth and the Moon, they're only about 30 feet thick in most places. That's like a giant hula hoop as wide as a city but as thin as a pizza!

17. Uranus has rings too, but they're harder to see than Saturn's. These rings are dark and thin, like skinny black hula hoops. Uranus also has 27

known moons, all named after characters from Shakespeare's plays. It's like a cosmic theater in space!

18. Neptune has a moon called Triton that orbits backwards. Scientists think Neptune "stole" Triton from somewhere else in space long ago. It's like Neptune won Triton in a cosmic game of catch!

19. Mercury has wrinkles! As the planet cooled down, its surface wrinkled up like a raisin. These wrinkles are actually long cliffs, some taller than the Grand Canyon. Imagine climbing a cliff made by a planet getting old!

20. Venus rotates so slowly that its day is longer than its year! It takes 225 Earth days for Venus to go around the Sun, but 243 Earth days to spin once. It's like Venus is doing a really, really slow dance around the Sun.

21. Earth is the only planet where we know water exists in all three states: solid (ice), liquid (water), and gas (water vapor). It's like Earth has a never-ending water cycle party going on all the time!

22. Mars has the largest dust storms in the solar system. They can last for months and cover the whole planet! It would be like having a giant, planet-wide sandbox that gets shaken up for weeks at a time.

23. Jupiter's Great Red Spot is shrinking! This giant storm has been raging for at least 400 years, but it's getting smaller. Scientists aren't sure why. It's like the biggest cosmic bathtub drain is slowly unplugging!

24. Saturn is the least dense planet in our solar system. It's so light that if you had a bathtub big enough, Saturn would float in it! Imagine a planet-sized rubber ducky bobbing in a cosmic bathtub.

25. Uranus was the first planet discovered using a telescope. Before that, people only knew about planets they could see with their eyes. It's like Uranus was playing hide and seek for thousands of years until someone invented a super eye to find it!

26. Neptune has the strongest winds in the solar system, but we're not sure why. Some areas have almost no wind, while others have super strong gusts. It's like Neptune can't decide if it wants to be a calm day or the stormiest planet ever!

27. Mercury has ice in some of its craters! Even though it's super close to the Sun, the bottoms of some craters never see sunlight, so they stay cold enough for ice. It's like finding popsicles in an oven!

28. Venus rotates in the opposite direction of most planets. If you could stand on Venus, you'd see the

Sun rise in the west and set in the east! It's like Venus decided to be different and spin the "wrong" way.

29. Earth is the only planet not named after a Greek or Roman god. All the other planets have fancy mythological names, but Earth just means "ground." It's like if all your friends had superhero names, but you were called "Kid."

30. Mars has the biggest volcano in the solar system, called Olympus Mons. It's three times taller than Mount Everest! If you stood on top, you'd be above most of Mars' atmosphere. It's like having a mountain so tall, it pokes out of the planet's air blanket!

Chapter Four

Moons: More Than Earth's Night Light

1. Moons are like planets' little buddies that follow them around in space. Some planets have lots of moons, while others have none. Earth has just

one moon, but Jupiter has 79 known moons! It's like Jupiter is the popular kid with a huge group of friends.

2. Our Moon is the fifth largest moon in the solar system. It's about one-quarter the size of Earth. If Earth was the size of a basketball, the Moon would be about as big as a tennis ball. That's still pretty big for a moon!

3. The Moon is the only place besides Earth where humans have walked. Twelve astronauts have been there, and they've left footprints that will last for millions of years because there's no wind to blow them away. It's like a permanent space museum of footprints!

4. The dark spots we see on the Moon are actually huge plains of hardened lava called "seas." But there's no water in them! Early astronomers thought they

were real seas, so the name stuck. It's like the Moon is playing a trick on us!

5. The Moon doesn't make its own light. What we see is sunlight bouncing off the Moon's surface. It's like the Moon is a giant mirror in the sky, reflecting the Sun's light back to us on Earth.

6. The Moon is slowly moving away from Earth at about 1.5 inches per year. That's about as fast as your fingernails grow! Don't worry, though - it won't float away. It's just scooting back a tiny bit each year.

7. Jupiter's moon Io is the most volcanic place in our solar system. It has hundreds of active volcanoes that shoot lava higher than Mount Everest! It's like Io is a cosmic fireworks show that never stops.

8. Saturn's moon Enceladus is covered in ice, but it shoots out giant water geysers from cracks in its surface. These geysers are so big, they feed Saturn's

rings! It's like Enceladus is a cosmic snow cone machine.

9. Jupiter's moon Europa might have more water than all of Earth's oceans combined! But it's all hidden under a thick layer of ice. Scientists think there might be life in Europa's ocean. It's like a giant space popsicle that might have surprises inside!

10. Saturn's largest moon, Titan, is the only moon known to have a thick atmosphere. It even has lakes, rivers, and rain, but they're made of liquid methane instead of water. It's like a bizarro Earth where everything is made of natural gas!

11. Our Moon always shows the same face to Earth. We never see the far side from the ground. It's not because the Moon is shy - it's just the way it rotates! It's like the Moon is playing a never-ending game of hide-and-seek with its far side.

12. Neptune's moon Triton is one of the coldest places in our solar system. Its surface is mostly frozen nitrogen, and it's so cold that nitrogen turns into ice! It's like a giant ball of cosmic ice cream that never melts.

13. Mars has two tiny moons named Phobos and Deimos. They're so small and oddly shaped that some scientists think they might be asteroids that Mars "caught" with its gravity. It's like Mars went fishing in space and caught two space rocks!

14. Jupiter's moon Ganymede is the largest moon in our solar system. It's even bigger than the planet Mercury! If Ganymede orbited the Sun instead of Jupiter, we might call it a planet. It's like the big kid in class who's taller than some adults.

15. Saturn's moon Mimas has a giant crater that makes it look like the Death Star from Star Wars.

The crater is called Herschel, and it takes up almost a third of Mimas' surface! It's like Mimas dressed up as a space station for cosmic Halloween.

16. Our Moon has "moonquakes" just like Earth has earthquakes. But Moon's quakes can last for hours because the Moon is so dry and cool inside. It's like the Moon gets the hiccups, but they take a really long time to go away!

17. Uranus has a moon named Miranda that looks like it was smashed to pieces and put back together wrong. It has cliffs, valleys, and weird patterns that don't match. It's like Miranda is a giant cosmic jigsaw puzzle that got mixed up.

18. Jupiter's moon Europa is covered in crisscrossing lines that make it look like a giant cracked egg. These lines are actually cracks in the icy surface where wa-

ter might bubble up from the ocean below. It's like Europa is a huge mosaic made of ice!

19. Saturn's moon Hyperion looks like a giant sponge floating in space. It's covered in deep craters that make it look holey and weird. Scientists aren't sure why it looks like this. It's like Hyperion is the Swiss cheese of the solar system!

20. Our Moon has no atmosphere, which means there's no air and no wind. That's why the astronauts' footprints are still there after all these years. It's like the Moon is a giant museum where nothing ever gets dusty or blown away.

21. Jupiter's moon Callisto is the most heavily cratered object in our solar system. Its entire surface is covered in craters of all sizes. It's like Callisto played cosmic dodgeball and got hit by every ball!

22. Saturn's rings are made up of billions of tiny moons - pieces of ice and rock ranging from the size of a grain of sand to as big as a house. It's like Saturn is wearing a giant, sparkly hula hoop made of mini-moons!

23. Earth's Moon is a quarter the size of our planet, which is huge for a moon! Most moons are tiny compared to their planets. It's like having a pet dog that's as big as a horse - pretty unusual!

24. Neptune's moon Triton orbits backwards compared to most moons. Scientists think Neptune might have "stolen" Triton from elsewhere in space long ago. It's like Triton is doing a silly backwards dance around Neptune!

25. Mars' moon Phobos is getting closer to Mars every year. In about 50 million years, it might crash into Mars or break apart to form a ring around the

planet. It's like Phobos and Mars are playing a very slow game of cosmic tag!

26. Jupiter's moon Io changes its looks more than any other object in the solar system. Its constant volcanic eruptions keep repainting its surface in reds, yellows, and oranges. It's like Io gets a new coat of paint every few months!

27. Saturn's moon Enceladus might have hot springs on its ocean floor, just like Earth does. These could provide energy and nutrients for potential life forms. It's like Enceladus might have its own tiny underwater alien spas!

28. Our Moon is slowly slowing down Earth's rotation. Long ago, Earth spun much faster and days were only about 6 hours long! In the very far future, a day on Earth might last 45 of our current days. It's like the Moon is a cosmic brake pedal for Earth!

29. Pluto's largest moon, Charon, is so big compared to Pluto that some scientists think they should be called a double dwarf planet system. They spin around each other like they're doing a space dance! It's like Pluto and Charon are holding hands while ice skating through space.

30. Some moons, like Saturn's Titan and Jupiter's Europa, might be better places to look for alien life than Mars! They have water, energy sources, and complex chemistry that could support life. It's like these moons are cosmic petri dishes where alien microbes might be growing!

Chapter Five

Asteroids, Comets, and Meteors: Space Rocks on the Move!

1. Asteroids, comets, and meteors are like the leftovers from when our solar system was made. They're bits and pieces that didn't become planets. It's like when you build with Lego, and you have extra pieces left over - these are the extra pieces of our solar system!

2. Asteroids are rocky space objects that orbit the Sun. They're smaller than planets but bigger than cars. Most asteroids live in the "asteroid belt" between Mars and Jupiter. It's like a cosmic rock collection floating in space!

3. Comets are balls of ice and dust that zoom around the Sun. When they get close to the Sun, the ice melts and makes a long, glowing tail. It's like a cosmic snowball leaving a trail of sparkles as it flies through space!

4. Meteors are what we call "shooting stars." They're actually tiny bits of space rock burning up in Earth's atmosphere. It's like nature's fireworks show! Most meteors are no bigger than a grain of sand.

5. The biggest asteroid we know is called Ceres. It's so big that scientists now call it a dwarf planet! Ceres is about 940 kilometers wide - that's like 20 New York Cities put together. It's the king of the asteroid belt!

6. Comets have two tails - one made of dust and one made of gas. The gas tail always points away from the Sun because of something called solar wind. It's like the Sun is blowing on the comet to make its tail!

7. Sometimes, lots of meteors appear at once in a "meteor shower." This happens when Earth passes through the dusty trail left by a comet. It's like Earth

is driving through a cosmic car wash made of tiny space rocks!

8. Asteroids can have mini moons! Some asteroids are big enough to have their own tiny asteroids orbiting them. It's like a parent asteroid taking its baby asteroid for a ride through space!

9. The most famous comet is called Halley's Comet. It visits Earth every 75-76 years. The last time we saw it was in 1986, and it will come back in 2061. It's like a cosmic friend that visits once in a lifetime!

10. If a meteor survives its trip through the atmosphere and lands on Earth, we call it a meteorite. People collect these space rocks! It's like finding a piece of outer space right here on Earth.

11. There's an asteroid named after Mr. Spock from Star Trek! It's called 2309 Mr. Spock. Scientists who discover asteroids get to name them, and sometimes

they pick fun names. It's like a cosmic fan club for favorite characters!

12. Comets are sometimes called "dirty snowballs" because they're made of ice, dust, and rocks. But they're not the kind of snowballs you'd want to throw! Some comets are as big as small towns.

13. The word "asteroid" means "star-like" in Greek. Early astronomers thought asteroids looked like tiny stars through their telescopes. But we now know they're not stars at all - they're space rocks! It's like a case of mistaken identity in space.

14. Some asteroids have rings, just like Saturn! The first asteroid found with rings is called Chariklo. It's like this asteroid wanted to dress up like a fancy planet and put on some cosmic jewelry!

15. Comets get their names from the people who discover them. Sometimes, computers spot comets

too! When that happens, the comet is named after the computer program. It's like giving a gold star to a robot for finding a cosmic snowball!

16. Meteors can make sounds as they zoom through the air. People have reported hearing hissing or booming sounds during big meteor events. It's like the meteors are trying to say "hello" as they fly by!

17. There's an asteroid shaped like a dog bone! It's called 216 Kleopatra, and it's about 217 kilometers long. Scientists think it might be made of metal. It's like a giant cosmic chew toy floating in space!

18. Some comets are so bright that you can see them during the day! These are called "Great Comets." The last one was in 2007, named Comet McNaught. It's like having a cosmic spotlight turn on in the middle of the day!

19. Meteorites are divided into three main types: iron, stone, and stony-iron. Iron meteorites are the heaviest and can be picked up with a magnet. It's like finding cosmic metal detectors are better at finding some space rocks than others!

20. There's a special group of asteroids called "Trojans" that follow planets in their orbits. Jupiter has the most Trojans - over 9,000! It's like these asteroids are playing "follow the leader" with planets.

21. Some comets break apart as they get close to the Sun. This happened to Comet Shoemaker-Levy 9, which then crashed into Jupiter in 1994. It was like watching cosmic fireworks as pieces of the comet hit the giant planet!

22. The fastest meteors can travel at speeds of 71 kilometers per second! That's like going from New

York to Los Angeles in less than a minute. These space speedsters really zoom through our sky!

23. There's an asteroid named after each member of the Beatles! There's 4147 Lennon, 4148 McCartney, 4149 Harrison, and 4150 Starr. It's like the Beatles have their own cosmic fan club in the asteroid belt!

24. Comets' tails can be super long. The record holder is Comet Hyakutake, whose tail stretched for about 570 million kilometers in 1996! That's like having a tail that could wrap around Earth 14,000 times!

25. Sometimes, meteors are bright enough to light up the whole sky! These are called "fireballs" or "bolides." It's like having a giant cosmic flashlight suddenly turn on above you!

26. Some asteroids have moons of their own! The first one discovered was Dactyl, which orbits the as-

teroid Ida. It's like some asteroids decided to start their own mini solar systems!

27. Comets smell bad! When scientists sniffed the artificial comet they made to study real ones, they said it smelled like rotten eggs, horse poop, and bitter almonds all mixed together. It's like comets are the stinky cheese of the solar system!

28. The biggest meteorite ever found on Earth is called Hoba. It weighs about 60 tons - as much as 10 big elephants! It's still where it landed in Namibia because it's too heavy to move. It's like Earth caught a giant cosmic bowling ball!

29. Some asteroids are so dark they reflect less light than charcoal! These are called C-type asteroids. It's like these asteroids are playing hide-and-seek with our telescopes, trying to stay invisible in space.

30. Comets might have brought water to Earth long ago! Some scientists think that when lots of comets hit early Earth, they delivered water that helped fill our oceans. It's like comets were cosmic water delivery trucks for baby Earth!

Chapter Six

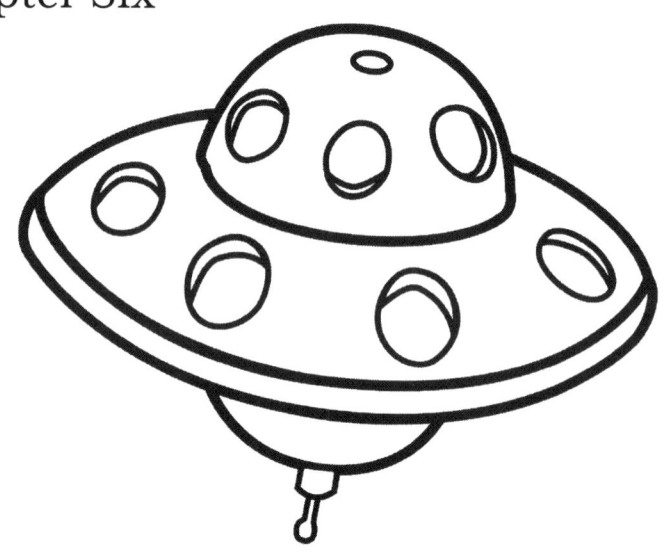

Aliens: Are We Alone in the Universe?

1. Aliens are beings that might live on other planets. We haven't found any yet, but scientists think there could be life out there because the universe is so big! It's like imagining a giant cosmic zoo filled with creatures we've never seen before.

2. Scientists use big radio telescopes to listen for alien signals from space. These huge "ears" try to hear any messages aliens might be sending. It's like trying to hear a whisper from really far away - we have to listen very carefully!

3. Some scientists think aliens might live on moons, not just planets! Moons like Jupiter's Europa or Saturn's Enceladus have oceans under their icy surfaces. Alien fish or space octopuses could be swimming in these far-away oceans!

4. The search for alien life is called SETI - it stands for Search for Extraterrestrial Intelligence. Scientists have been doing SETI for over 60 years! It's like a really long game of hide-and-seek where we're still looking for the aliens.

5. If aliens exist, they might not look like us at all! They could be as small as bacteria or as big as moun-

tains. Some might have tentacles, or six eyes, or be made of gas! It's like imagining the weirdest creature you can think of - aliens could be even weirder!

6. One way we look for aliens is by searching for "exoplanets" - planets around other stars. We've found thousands of them! Some of these planets might be just right for life, like Earth. It's like house-hunting for aliens in space!

7. Scientists think that if we find alien life, it will probably be tiny microbes first, not big green aliens in spaceships. These microbes might live on Mars or on moons in our solar system. It's like looking for alien germs instead of alien people!

8. The famous SETI scientist Frank Drake came up with an equation to guess how many alien civilizations might be out there. It's called the Drake Equa-

tion. It's like a math problem to count aliens we haven't even found yet!

9. Some people think aliens have visited Earth in UFOs (Unidentified Flying Objects). Scientists say there's no proof of this, but it's fun to imagine! It's like thinking your new neighbor might secretly be from another planet.

10. If we ever meet aliens, we might not be able to talk to them easily. They probably won't speak English or any Earth language! Scientists have thought about using math or pictures to communicate. It's like trying to play charades with someone from another galaxy!

11. In movies and books, aliens often come to Earth in flying saucers. But real scientists think alien spaceships (if they exist) could look totally different. They might use technology we can't even imagine yet! It's

like trying to guess what cars will look like 1000 years from now.

12. Some planets and moons in our solar system might have the ingredients for life, like water and heat. Mars, Europa, and Enceladus are some of the places scientists are most excited about. It's like having a cosmic cookbook and looking for places with the right ingredients for alien life!

13. If aliens sent us a message, it might take a very long time to reach us. Radio waves travel at the speed of light, but space is huge! A message from the nearest star would take over 4 years to get here. It's like waiting for a letter that takes years to arrive!

14. Scientists have sent messages into space for aliens to find. One famous message is on golden records attached to the Voyager spacecraft. These records have

sounds and pictures from Earth. It's like sending a cosmic postcard to alien pen pals!

15. Some scientists worry that if we find aliens, they might not be friendly. Others think advanced aliens would be peaceful. We just don't know! It's like wondering if the new kid in school will be nice or mean before you meet them.

16. The idea of life on Mars has been popular for a long time. In 1877, an astronomer thought he saw canals on Mars and people imagined Martians built them! We now know there are no canals, but we're still looking for tiny Martian microbes.

17. If we find alien life, it might not need the same things we do to survive. Some scientists think there could be life based on different chemistry than life on Earth. It's like imagining animals that don't need to eat or breathe like we do!

18. The Fermi Paradox is a famous idea about aliens. It asks: if there are lots of aliens out there, why haven't we seen them yet? It's like wondering why you can't find any unicorns if they're supposed to be real.

19. Some scientists have suggested using laser beams to send messages to aliens. These light signals could be seen from very far away. It's like using a giant cosmic flashlight to say "hello" to ET!

20. In science fiction stories, aliens often have special powers like telepathy or the ability to shape-shift. While we don't know if real aliens would have powers, it's fun to imagine! It's like dreaming up your own alien superhero.

21. The "Zoo Hypothesis" is an idea that aliens might be watching us but not contacting us, like we're animals in a zoo. Some scientists think this

could explain why we haven't heard from aliens yet. It's like being in a big cosmic wildlife park!

22. If we do find alien life, scientists have plans to make sure we don't contaminate it with Earth germs, or that it doesn't contaminate us. It's like having special rules for the cleanest playdate ever, but with alien microbes!

23. Some scientists think that if alien civilizations exist, they might build huge structures in space that we could see. These are called "megastructures." It's like looking for alien skyscrapers so big we can see them from other stars!

24. The famous scientist Stephen Hawking warned that meeting aliens might be dangerous for humans. He thought they might want our resources. But other scientists disagree. It's like debating whether to say hi to the new neighbors or hide from them!

25. There's a special scale called the Rio Scale that measures how exciting an alien discovery would be. Finding a radio signal from aliens would be super high on this scale! It's like having a special thermometer that measures how cool alien news is.

26. Some people think crop circles are made by aliens, but most are actually made by humans as art or pranks. Scientists say aliens probably wouldn't make shapes in our fields to say hello. It's like thinking your cat is writing you messages when it scratches the furniture!

27. If aliens visited Earth a long time ago, they might have left something behind. Some people look for signs of ancient aliens, but scientists haven't found any real proof. It's like being a detective looking for clues from space visitors who might have come millions of years ago!

28. Tardigrades, tiny animals also called "water bears," can survive in space! Some scientists think creatures like these could travel between planets on asteroids. It's like imagining the toughest, tiniest astronauts hitching rides on space rocks!

29. Some scientists have suggested that we might BE the aliens! The idea is that life on Earth could have started from microbes that came here on comets or asteroids. It's like finding out you're adopted, but on a whole planet scale!

30. Even if we don't find aliens soon, searching for them helps us learn more about our universe and our place in it. It makes us ask big questions about life and what it means to not be alone. It's like going on a cosmic adventure that teaches us about ourselves!

Chapter Seven

Black Holes: The Universe's Most Mysterious Monsters

:

1. Black holes are like cosmic vacuum cleaners. They have such strong gravity that nothing, not even light, can escape once it gets too close! It's like a giant space whirlpool that sucks in everything nearby. But don't worry, black holes are very far away from Earth!

2. Black holes form when really big stars die. The star explodes, and then all its leftovers squish down into a tiny space. It's like taking a huge beach ball and squeezing it until it's smaller than a grain of sand!

3. The edge of a black hole is called the "event horizon." It's the point of no return - once something crosses it, it can't get out. It's like a cosmic slide that only goes down, never up!

4. Time moves differently near a black hole. If you could watch someone fall into a black hole, they'd seem to slow down and freeze at the edge. But for the

person falling in, time would seem normal. It's like a weird space magic trick!

5. Black holes can be tiny or super huge. The smallest might be as small as an atom, but the biggest are millions of times heavier than our Sun! It's like comparing a pea to a whole planet - that's how much black holes can differ in size.

6. Scientists think there's a supermassive black hole at the center of our galaxy, the Milky Way. It's called Sagittarius A*, and it's 4 million times heavier than our Sun! It's like having a cosmic giant living in the middle of our galactic neighborhood.

7. Black holes aren't really black! They can glow because of all the hot stuff swirling around them before it falls in. This glowing disk is called an "accretion disk." It's like a cosmic light show put on by the hungriest thing in the universe!

8. If Earth were squished into a black hole, it would be about the size of a peanut. But it would still weigh the same as Earth! It's like magic shrinking ray that makes things tiny but keeps them just as heavy.

9. Black holes can shoot out powerful jets of energy and matter from their poles. These jets can be longer than whole galaxies! It's like the black hole is a cosmic fire hose, spraying energy across space.

10. Einstein's theory of general relativity helped us understand black holes. But Einstein himself didn't believe they could really exist! It's like inventing a recipe for the world's best cookie, but thinking no one could ever actually bake it.

11. Black holes aren't cosmic vacuum cleaners that suck in everything. If our Sun turned into a black hole right now (which it won't!), Earth would keep

orbiting it just like before. It's like changing a light bulb - it doesn't make all the furniture fly towards it!

12. Some scientists think really tiny black holes might have formed right after the Big Bang. These are called "primordial black holes." They could be as small as atoms but as heavy as mountains! It's like having cosmic marbles that weigh as much as hills.

13. Black holes can merge together. When they do, they send out ripples in space called gravitational waves. Scientists detected these waves for the first time in 2015! It's like hearing the "splash" when two cosmic cannonballs fall into a space pool.

14. If you fell into a big black hole, you'd get stretched out like spaghetti! Scientists call this "spaghettification." It's like being pulled apart by the strongest cosmic taffy puller ever!

15. Some black holes spin really fast. The fastest ones might spin nearly as fast as the speed of light! It's like a cosmic merry-go-round that's spinning so fast, it's almost a blur.

16. We can't see black holes directly, but we can see how they affect things around them. It's like seeing a invisible kid on a swing - you can't see the kid, but you can see the swing moving!

17. Some scientists think there might be wormholes inside black holes. These could be like tunnels to other parts of the universe or even other universes! It's like having a secret cosmic shortcut hidden inside the scariest thing in space.

18. The biggest black hole we know of is called TON 618. It's 66 billion times heavier than our Sun! That's like comparing a tiny ant to a whole herd of ele-

phants - TON 618 is that much bigger than other black holes.

19. Black holes don't just pull things in - they can also spit things out! This is called Hawking radiation, named after the scientist Stephen Hawking. It's like the black hole is slowly leaking, but it takes a really, really long time.

20. If you could somehow survive inside a black hole, you might see the future of the entire universe flash before your eyes! This is because of how black holes bend time and space. It's like having a magical snow globe that shows you everything that will ever happen!

21. Black holes can make stars move in weird ways. By watching stars zoom around nothing, scientists found the black hole at the center of our galaxy. It's

like seeing invisible cosmic puppeteer pulling on star strings!

22. Some scientists think that inside a black hole, the laws of physics might break down. We don't know what would happen then! It's like imagining a place where the rules of a board game suddenly don't work anymore.

23. Black holes don't live forever. Over a very, very long time, they slowly evaporate through Hawking radiation. But for big black holes, this takes much longer than the current age of the universe! It's like a cosmic ice cube that takes trillions of years to melt.

24. There might be millions of black holes in our galaxy that we can't see. They're just floating around space, invisible to us. It's like playing hide and seek with cosmic monsters that are really, really good at hiding!

25. Light bends around black holes because of their strong gravity. This bending can act like a giant magnifying glass in space, letting us see far-away things more clearly. It's like the black hole is wearing giant cosmic glasses!

26. If you shine a flashlight near a black hole, the light might orbit the black hole instead of going straight! The black hole's gravity is so strong it can make light go in circles. It's like playing catch with a beam of light around a cosmic maypole!

27. Some scientists think that when the universe ends, it might turn into a giant black hole. Everything would get sucked in! But don't worry, if this happens, it won't be for trillions and trillions of years. It's like the ultimate cosmic clean-up at the end of the universe's party.

28. Black holes can make really loud "sounds," but we can't hear them in space. NASA changed these sounds so we can hear them, and they sound super spooky! It's like the black hole is singing the scariest lullaby ever.

29. Some black holes are "sleeping giants." They're not eating anything right now, so they're hard to find. But if they start eating stars or gas, they'll wake up and glow brightly! It's like cosmic dragons that sleep for millions of years before waking up hungry.

30. Scientists took the first-ever picture of a black hole in 2019! It looks like a glowing orange donut. The black hole is actually the dark part in the middle. It's like finally seeing a photo of the universe's shyest monster!

Chapter Eight

Galaxies: Giant Star Cities Across the Universe

1. Galaxies are like giant cosmic cities made of stars, gas, dust, and dark matter. Our galaxy, the Milky Way, has over 100 billion stars! That's more stars than there are grains of sand on all of Earth's beaches. Imagine a sand castle as big as the universe!

2. The Milky Way looks like a milky band across the night sky. Ancient Greeks thought it looked like spilled milk, so they called it the "galaxy," which means "milky" in Greek. It's like someone spilled a giant glass of star milk across the sky!

3. There are three main types of galaxies: spiral (like pinwheels), elliptical (like cosmic footballs), and irregular (like cosmic blobs). Our Milky Way is a spiral galaxy. It's like the universe has different shapes of cosmic Lego bricks to build with!

4. The closest big galaxy to us is called Andromeda. It's so big that if it were brighter, it would look six

times wider than the full moon in our sky! It's like having a cosmic neighbor's house that's bigger than your whole town.

5. Galaxies can crash into each other! When this happens, it's called a galactic collision. Don't worry, stars rarely bump into each other because space is so big. It's like mixing two jars of glitter - the glitter pieces don't hit each other, they just blend together.

6. The biggest galaxy we know is called IC 1101. It's over 50 times bigger than our Milky Way! If the Milky Way were the size of a quarter, IC 1101 would be as big as a bicycle wheel. That's one huge cosmic city!

7. Most galaxies have a supermassive black hole at their center. These black holes can be millions or billions of times heavier than our Sun. It's like each

galaxy has a cosmic monster living in its downtown area!

8. Galaxies come in different colors. Younger galaxies with lots of new stars look blue, while older galaxies with older stars look redder. It's like galaxies change hair color as they get older, just like some people do!

9. Our Milky Way galaxy is about 100,000 light-years across. That means it would take light, the fastest thing in the universe, 100,000 years to travel from one side to the other! It's like having a race track so big it takes 100,000 years to run across.

10. Galaxies are grouped together in clusters. Our Milky Way is part of a small cluster called the Local Group. It's like galaxies have their own neighborhoods and friend groups in space!

11. The space between galaxies isn't empty - it's filled with hot gas. This gas is so hot that it glows with

X-rays! It's like the universe has a cosmic hot tub between its galaxy islands.

12. Some galaxies are shaped like rings. These ring galaxies probably formed when one galaxy punched through the middle of another one! It's like the universe is playing a giant game of cosmic ring toss.

13. There's a galaxy called the Sombrero Galaxy because it looks like a giant hat in space. It has a bright, bulging center surrounded by thin, glowing rings of stars. It's like the universe decided to dress up and put on a fancy cosmic sombrero!

14. Scientists think there are over 100 billion galaxies in the observable universe. That's as many galaxies as there are stars in our Milky Way! It's like having a jar of cosmic jellybeans where each jellybean is actually a jar with billions more jellybeans inside.

15. Some galaxies are actively making lots of new stars. We call these starburst galaxies. They're like cosmic star factories working overtime to produce shiny new stars!

16. Our Milky Way galaxy is moving through space at about 1.3 million miles per hour! But don't worry, we can't feel it because everything in the galaxy is moving together. It's like being on a super-fast cosmic train, but everything inside the train seems still.

17. The oldest galaxy we've seen so far is about 13.4 billion years old. That's almost as old as the universe itself! It's like finding a cosmic great-great-great-grandparent of our Milky Way.

18. Dwarf galaxies are like the cosmic kids of the galaxy world. They're much smaller than regular galaxies, with only a few billion stars. Our Milky

Way has over 20 dwarf galaxies orbiting it, like little cosmic moons!

19. The Milky Way and Andromeda galaxies are moving towards each other. In about 4 billion years, they'll collide and merge into one big galaxy! It's like a very slow-motion game of cosmic bumper cars that takes billions of years to play.

20. Some galaxies shoot out huge jets of energy from their centers. These are called active galaxies. It's like these galaxies have cosmic fire hoses blasting energy into space!

21. There's a galaxy called the Cartwheel Galaxy that looks like a giant wheel in space. It got its shape from a galactic collision millions of years ago. It's like the universe played cosmic Frisbee and made a galaxy-sized wheel!

22. Galaxies can have spiral arms, but these arms aren't solid things. They're areas where there are more stars and gas. As the galaxy spins, the arms keep their shape. It's like a cosmic pinwheel that keeps its pattern as it spins!

23. There's a type of galaxy called a lenticular galaxy. It's like a mix between a spiral and an elliptical galaxy. They're shaped like cosmic frisbees! It's like the universe couldn't decide between making a pinwheel or a football, so it made something in between.

24. Our Milky Way galaxy is warped, like a bent record. Scientists think this might be because of our galaxy bumping into smaller galaxies in the past. It's like our galaxy is a cosmic potato chip that got a little bent!

25. The stars at the edge of our galaxy take about 250 million years to go around the center once. We call

this a cosmic year. Dinosaurs lived during a different cosmic year than us! It's like the galaxy has its own super-slow clock.

26. Some galaxies are so far away that their light takes billions of years to reach us. When we look at them, we're seeing them as they were billions of years ago! It's like having a time machine telescope that lets us see baby pictures of galaxies.

27. There are galaxies called "green pea" galaxies because they look small and green. They're forming stars super fast and are very rare. It's like finding a four-leaf clover in a field of cosmic clovers!

28. Our galaxy, the Milky Way, is eating smaller galaxies right now! It's pulling in stars and gas from its dwarf galaxy neighbors. It's like our galaxy is having a very slow cosmic lunch that takes millions of years to eat.

29. There's a galaxy called Hoag's Object that looks like a perfect ring with a ball in the middle. Scientists aren't sure how it formed. It's like finding a perfect cosmic donut floating in space!

30. The light from all the stars in all the galaxies in the universe adds up to make a faint glow called the cosmic optical background. It's like all the galaxies together make one big, soft cosmic night light for the universe!

Chapter Nine

Spaceships and Rovers: Exploring the Final Frontier

1. Rockets are like giant space bottles with their caps popped off! They shoot out hot gas at the bottom,

which pushes them up into space. It's like sitting on a super-powered bouncy ball that can jump all the way to the stars!

2. The first human-made object to reach space was a V-2 rocket in 1944. But it wasn't trying to explore - it was a weapon in World War II. Scientists later used similar rockets for peaceful space exploration. It's like turning a water gun into a garden hose!

3. Yuri Gagarin was the first person in space in 1961. His spaceship, Vostok 1, was like a tiny apartment - just big enough for one person! He orbited Earth once in 108 minutes. That's like going around the whole world faster than you can watch a movie!

4. The Apollo missions took humans to the Moon. The spacecraft had three parts: the command module (like the driver's seat), the service module (like the engine), and the lunar module (like a cosmic

rowboat to land on the Moon). It was like a cosmic Swiss Army knife!

5. Space shuttles were like cosmic pickup trucks. They could go to space, drop off satellites or astronauts, and then land back on Earth like an airplane. They were used 135 times between 1981 and 2011. That's a lot of space deliveries!

6. The International Space Station (ISS) is like a giant space house. It's been occupied by humans continuously since 2000. Astronauts live and work there, doing experiments in space. It's like a cosmic laboratory that's always floating above our heads!

7. Mars rovers are like remote-controlled cars on Mars. They have cameras, robot arms, and science tools to study the Red Planet. The latest one, Perseverance, even has a tiny helicopter called Ingenu-

ity! It's like sending a cosmic explorer kit to another world.

8. The Hubble Space Telescope is like a big space camera. It orbits Earth and takes super clear pictures of distant stars and galaxies. It's been working since 1990! Imagine having a camera so good it can see billions of light-years away.

9. The Voyager spacecraft are the farthest human-made objects from Earth. They've been traveling for over 40 years and have left our solar system! They carry golden records with sounds and pictures from Earth. It's like sending a cosmic postcard to alien civilizations.

10. SpaceX's Falcon rockets can land back on Earth after launching into space. They land standing up on their rocket engines! It's like throwing a pencil in the air and having it land perfectly standing on its eraser.

11. The Curiosity rover on Mars is as big as a car and uses a nuclear battery. It's been exploring Mars since 2012, climbing mountains and digging in the dirt. It's like having a nuclear-powered robot geologist on another planet!

12. The James Webb Space Telescope has a giant mirror made of 18 smaller mirrors. It's so big it had to fold up like origami to fit in the rocket! Now it's in space, taking pictures of the oldest galaxies. It's like having cosmic binoculars that can see the past!

13. The Parker Solar Probe is studying the Sun up close. It gets so close that it flies through the Sun's outer atmosphere! It has a special shield to protect it from the extreme heat. It's like a cosmic marshmallow toaster, but for science!

14. The Cassini spacecraft explored Saturn for 13 years. At the end of its mission, scientists crashed it

into Saturn so it wouldn't hit Saturn's moons. It's like cleaning up after a cosmic party - Cassini took itself out with the trash!

15. The New Horizons spacecraft flew by Pluto in 2015, giving us our first close-up pictures of this distant world. It's still going, exploring even farther objects. It's like a cosmic tourist taking pictures of the solar system's farthest attractions!

16. The Ingenuity helicopter on Mars is the first aircraft to fly on another planet! It's super light and has specially designed blades to fly in Mars' thin atmosphere. It's like having a cosmic drone explorer on the Red Planet!

17. The Chinese rover Yutu-2 is exploring the far side of the Moon. It's the first rover to land on the side of the Moon we can't see from Earth. It's like

having a cosmic explorer peek behind the Moon's curtain!

18. The OSIRIS-REx spacecraft grabbed a sample from an asteroid named Bennu. It's bringing the sample back to Earth for scientists to study. It's like playing a game of cosmic tag, but instead of just touching the asteroid, it brought a piece home!

19. The Juno spacecraft is orbiting Jupiter, studying the giant planet's storms and magnetic field. It's powered by solar panels, even though Jupiter is really far from the Sun. It's like running a cosmic science lab on really long extension cords!

20. The Tianhe module is the core of China's new space station. More modules will be added to make a complete station where astronauts can live and work. It's like building a cosmic Lego set, one piece at a time in space!

21. The Dream Chaser is a new spacecraft that looks like a mini space shuttle. It's designed to carry cargo to the International Space Station and land on a runway like an airplane. It's like a cosmic delivery truck that can parallel park!

22. The Psyche mission will explore an asteroid made mostly of metal. Scientists think it might be the exposed core of an early planet. It's like finding a cosmic fossil of a baby planet that never grew up!

23. The Mars Helicopter Ingenuity has solar panels to charge its batteries and a tiny heater to stay warm in the cold Martian nights. It's like a cosmic cell phone that needs to plug in and bundle up every night!

24. The Dragonfly mission will send a drone-like aircraft to explore Saturn's moon Titan. Titan has lakes and seas, but they're filled with liquid methane, not

water! It's like sending a cosmic seaplane to explore an alien ocean.

25. The Artemis program aims to send humans back to the Moon, including the first woman and person of color to walk on the lunar surface. They'll use a new big rocket called the Space Launch System. It's like planning a cosmic field trip with the biggest school bus ever!

26. The ExoMars rover, Rosalind Franklin, will drill deep into Mars' surface to look for signs of past life. It's like giving Mars a check-up with a cosmic dentist drill!

27. The VIPER rover will explore the Moon's south pole, looking for water ice. If it finds a lot, future astronauts might be able to use it. It's like a cosmic prospector looking for moon gold, but the gold is actually ice!

28. The Nancy Grace Roman Space Telescope will study dark energy and look for new planets. Its camera is so powerful it's like taking a picture of a penny from 40 kilometers away! That's some serious cosmic zoom.

29. The JUICE mission will explore Jupiter's icy moons. Scientists think these moons might have oceans under their icy surfaces where alien life could exist. It's like a cosmic submarine mission, but the submarine is actually a spacecraft!

30. Future spacecraft might use ion engines, which shoot out tiny particles really fast to move. They're super efficient but provide only a little push. It's like moving through space by blowing really hard through a straw - slow but steady!

Chapter Ten

Becoming a Space Explorer: Your Future in the Stars

1. Astronauts are like space sailors who explore the cosmic ocean. They fly in spaceships, do experiments in zero gravity, and sometimes even walk on other worlds! To become an astronaut, you need to study

hard, especially math and science. It's like training to be a superhero, but for real!

2. Astronomers are like space detectives. They use big telescopes to look at stars, planets, and galaxies far away. They solve cosmic mysteries and discover new things in space all the time. If you love stargazing and asking big questions, you might want to be an astronomer when you grow up!

3. Space engineers are like cosmic inventors. They design and build spaceships, rovers, and satellites. They figure out how to make things work in space where there's no air and things float around. It's like being a wizard who makes magic space machines!

4. Did you know that you can start training to be a space explorer right now? Learn about space, do science experiments, and stay healthy. NASA has a kids' club where you can play space games and learn

cool stuff. It's like having a cosmic clubhouse in your computer!

5. In the future, we might have hotels in space! Companies are already planning space stations where tourists can visit. Imagine having a vacation where you float around and see Earth from space. It would be like the coolest field trip ever!

6. Scientists are working on building a base on the Moon. Future astronauts might live there for months at a time. They'll do experiments, explore the Moon, and learn how to live on another world. It's like building a cosmic treehouse, but on the Moon!

7. To go to space, astronauts have to be in really good shape. They exercise for two hours every day, even in space! They use special machines to keep their mus-

cles strong in zero gravity. It's like having a floating gym in space!

8. Space food has come a long way since the first astronauts. Now, astronauts can eat things like tacos, ice cream, and even pizza in space! But they have to be careful not to let their food float away. It's like having a picnic where everything wants to fly!

9. In the future, we might grow food on Mars! Scientists are figuring out how to grow plants in Mars-like soil. Astronauts might be the first farmers on another planet. It's like having a cosmic vegetable garden millions of miles from Earth!

10. Space suits are like personal spaceships. They keep astronauts safe in space where there's no air and it's really cold or hot. Future space suits for Mars might be more flexible and easier to move in. It's like

wearing a high-tech onesie that protects you from space!

11. Kids can help space exploration right now by being citizen scientists. You can count craters on the Moon, spot changes on Mars, or even help find new planets! It's like being a space explorer from your own home.

12. In the future, we might mine asteroids for valuable materials. Some asteroids have lots of metals that are rare on Earth. It would be like a cosmic treasure hunt, looking for space gold and platinum!

13. Scientists are working on new rockets that could take us to Mars faster. Some ideas include nuclear-powered rockets or ones that use electricity. It's like inventing a cosmic race car to zoom through space!

14. Future space explorers might use 3D printers to make things they need in space. Forgot your toothbrush? Just print a new one! It's like having a magic wand that can create any tool you need, even on Mars.

15. One day, we might build a giant elevator to space! It would be a cable stretching from Earth all the way up to orbit. You could ride it to space instead of using a rocket. It's like having a cosmic escalator to the stars!

16. Space scientists are looking for places where aliens might live. They're especially interested in moons with oceans under their icy surfaces. Future explorers might dive into these alien oceans in special submarines. It's like being a cosmic Jacques Cousteau!

17. To become a space scientist, you don't just need to be good at science. You also need to be creative, work well with others, and never give up when things get tough. It's like being part scientist, part artist, and part superhero!

18. In the future, we might have races on the Moon! With the Moon's low gravity, you could jump really high and far. Imagine playing basketball where you can easily dunk from half-court. It would be like sports in a giant bouncy castle!

19. Space explorers of the future might use virtual reality to feel like they're on other planets before they go there. They could practice driving Mars rovers or walking on the Moon. It's like having the coolest video game ever, but it helps you prepare for real space missions!

20. Scientists are working on ways to protect astronauts from space radiation on long trips. One idea is to use force fields, just like in science fiction movies! It's like having an invisible umbrella that protects you from cosmic rays.

21. Future Moon explorers might live in houses made of Moon dirt! Scientists are figuring out how to turn Moon dust into building materials. It's like making cosmic sandcastles that you can live in!

22. Space archaeologists study the things humans have left in space, like old satellites or Moon landing sites. They help preserve space history. It's like being Indiana Jones, but instead of exploring ancient temples, you explore the history of space exploration!

23. In the future, we might have space gas stations! Spacecraft could stop and refuel on their way to

Mars or other planets. It's like a cosmic road trip, complete with pit stops to fill up the tank.

24. Some scientists think we should send tiny spacecraft to explore other star systems. These would be powered by giant lasers pushing on light sails. It's like cosmic sailboats racing to other stars!

25. Future Mars explorers might live in giant domes that protect them from the harsh Martian environment. These could have parks, houses, and even swimming pools inside! It's like building a cosmic snow globe that people can live in.

26. Space lawyers help make rules for space exploration. They work on things like who owns the Moon or what happens if a satellite crashes. It's like being a cosmic referee, making sure everyone plays fair in space!

27. In the future, we might have space factories. Some things are easier to make in zero gravity, like perfect crystals or special medicines. It's like having a cosmic workshop where you can make things you can't make on Earth!

28. Space explorers of the future might use hibernation pods for long trips. They would sleep for months or years while traveling to far planets. It's like taking the longest nap ever while your spaceship does all the driving!

29. Some people think we should terraform Mars - change it to be more like Earth. This would take hundreds of years but could give Mars air to breathe and water to drink. It's like giving a whole planet a makeover!

30. Future space suits might be as thin as regular clothes but still protect astronauts. They could

change color to absorb or reflect heat as needed. It's like wearing magical pyjamas that keep you safe in space!

31. Kids today might be the first humans to walk on Mars! If you're in elementary school now, you could be the right age to join a Mars mission when you grow up. It's like being part of the biggest adventure in human history. Dream big and reach for the stars!